E&D Primary English Course

PUPIL'S BOOK

Revised Edition

Maria Lwendo, M.G. Kihampa, Remeny Mnzava Kristeen Oberlander Chachage

E & D Vision Publishing
Dar es Salaam

E&D Vision Publishing Limited
P.O. Box 4460
Dar es Salaam
Email: info@edvisionpublishing.co.tz
Website: www.edvisionpublishing.co.tz

© M. Lwendo, M.G. Kihampa, R. Mnzava,
Kristeen Oberlander Chachage, 2006.
3rd Edition, 2014

Illustrator: Abdul Gugu
Page layout & design: Ajik Designs

ISBN 9987 622 14 3

UNITED REPUBLIC OF TANZANIA
MINISTRY OF EDUCATION AND VOCATIONAL TRAINING

Certificate of Approval
NO. 650

Title of Publication: E&D Primary English Course 1 (PB)
Author: Maria Lwendo et al.
Publisher: E&D Limited
ISBN: 9987 622 14 3
This book was approved by EMAC on 8 (date) 1 (month) 2007 (year) to be a Course Book for Standard 1 in **Primary Schools** in Tanzania as per 20 05 Syllabus.

R. A. Mpama
CHAIRPERSON
EMAC   SEAL

All rights reserved. No part of this book may be reproduced in any form without written permission of E & D Vision Publishing Limited.

About the Authors

Maria Lwendo is a nursery and grade one teacher. She has a teaching diploma with 15 years experience in Kenya and Tanzania, in government and private English - medium schools, at nursery, primary and secondary levels.

M.G. Kihampa a retired teacher has 19 years teaching experience and 15 years as a school inspector. She holds a diploma of education, she has authored several children's readers.

Remeny Mnzava has 20 years English teaching experience in and outside Tanzania, in primary, secondary and teacher education. She holds a diploma in education. She is the founder of Mami Early Learning Centre.

Series Editor & Coordinator

Kristeen Oberlander Chachage, the writing coordinator and series editor, has an MA in teaching and curriculum in teaching English to speakers of other languages. She has a substantive teaching experience in Tanzania at primary, secondary and university levels. Currently she is a teacher trainer and lecturer in teaching English as a second language.

Table of Contents

UNIT	TITLE	PAGE
1	How are you?	1
2	Boys and Girls	8
3	A New Friend	12
4	Name It	16
5	Meet my family	21
6	Rehema Can Read	26
7	Let us Count	30
8	Cat and Mouse	37
9	The Kitten and her Milk	41
10	The Lost Goats	47
11	Lion and Mouse	55
12	Let us Play a Game	61
13	Days of the Week	65
14	Amani and the Rabbit	69
15	Count to Fifty	74
16	What is Happening?	79

Standard One Keywords 85

Unit 1 How are you?

mother   father   teacher

Rehema   Amani   class

Sing!

Good morning to you
Good morning to you
Good morning dear teacher,
Good morning to you

Good morning to you
Good morning to you
Good morning dear teacher,
Good morning to you

Good afternoon to you
Good afternoon to you
Good afternoon dear teacher,
Good afternoon to you

Good evening to you
Good evening to you
Good evening dear mother,
Good evening to you

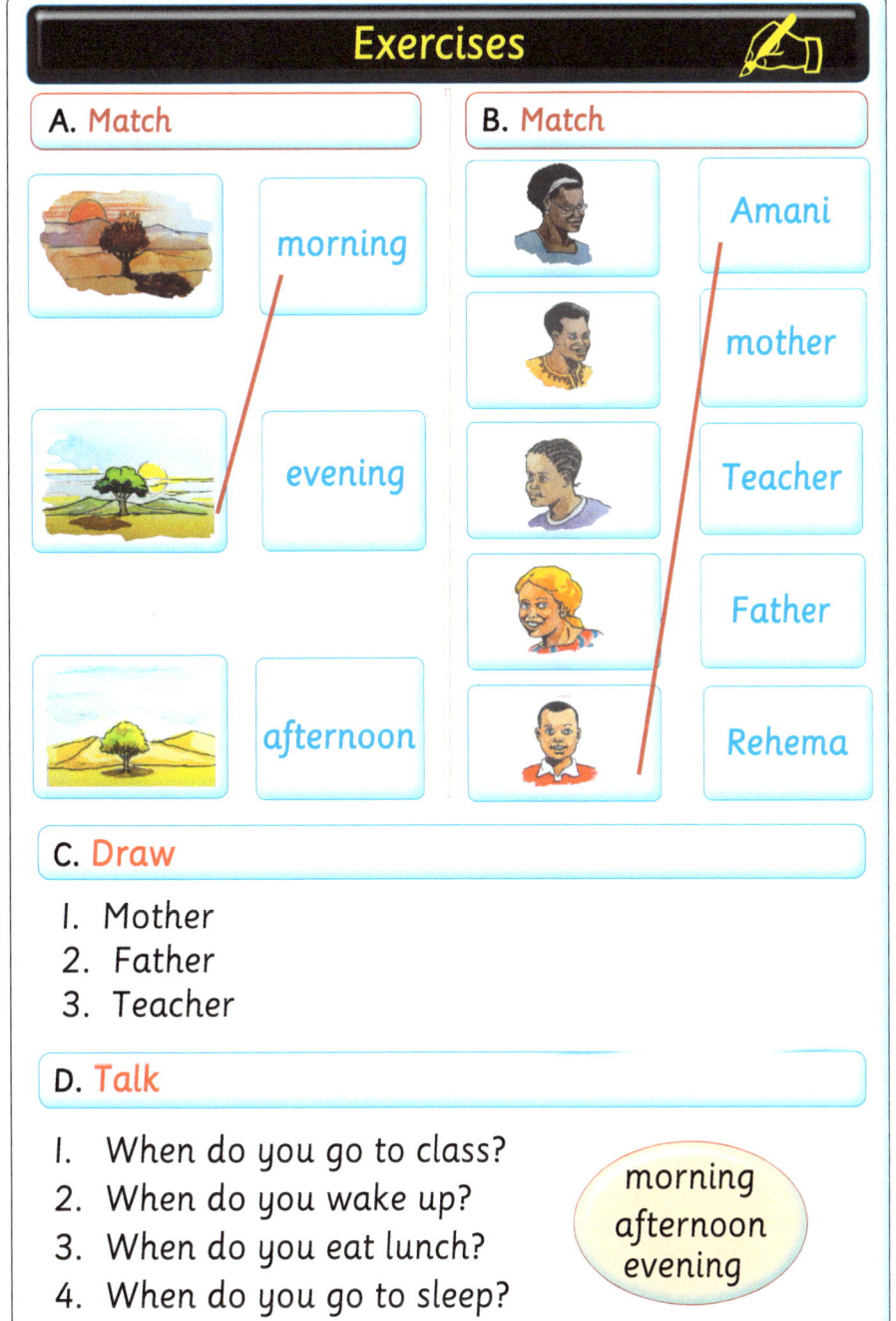

Unit 2 Boys and Girls

girl

boy

Tell us about yourself

My name is ....

I am a .... [boy/girl]

This is me. (draw!)

Exercises

A. Say the right one.

He is a boy / She is a girl

Rehema   Faraja   Zawadi   Amani

B. Say she or he

She / He

1. ....is a girl.
2. ....is a boy.
3. ....is a teacher.
4. ....is a father.
5. ....is a mother.

Unit 3 A new friend

Exercises

A. Read

My name is Amani.
I am a boy.
I am 7 years old.
I am a pupil.

My name is Zawadi.
I am a girl.
I am 8 years old.
I am a pupil.

B. Copy and fill in the gaps

Faraja   Zawadi   Amani   Rehema

Example: His name is ...Faraja......

Her name is ....

Her name is ....

His name is ....

C. Write the answer. Choose Yes or No

Yes / No

Is she a boy?

Is he a boy?

Is she a girl?

Is she a teacher?

Is he a girl?

C. Write the answers about yourself

Yes / No

Are you a boy?

Are you a girl?

Are you a teacher?

Are you a friend?

Poem

Tell me little one who are you?
I am a tiny winy little dog.
And you my friend,
Who are you?

Telephone

Hello!
How are you?
Are you Rehema?
Rehema, how is your mother?
How is your father?
Goodbye!

Hello!
I am fine, thank you.
Yes, I am.
She is fine.
He is fine, thank you.
Goodbye!

Make a telephone

Unit 4 Name It

This and that

Exercises

A. What is this?

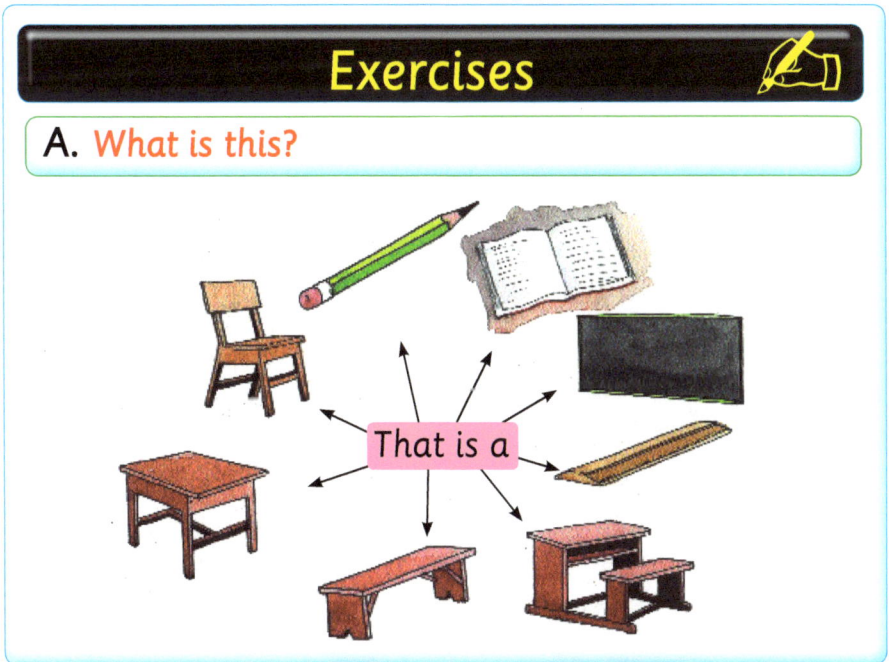

That is a

B. What is that?

book, pencil, bench, chair, table, blackboard, tree.

That is a ....
That is a ....
That is a ....
That is a ....
That is a ....
That is a ....
That is a ....

C. Find the odd one out

D. Name these things

t	ch	p	be ....
h	tr	bi	st ....
bl	d	r	b ....

table   pencil   stone   blackboard   tree   bench
chair   book   house   ruler   bicycle   desk

E. Copy and fill in the gaps

chair   book   pencil   bicycle

1. Read the...............................
2. Sit on the.............................
3. Write with the........................
4. Ride the ....

Revision

A. Read

I am a pupil.
You are a girl.
She is a teacher.
He is a boy.

B. Match and write

I — is
He — am
She — are
You — is

C. What do the say?

Evening

Afternoon

Morning

Unit 5 Meet my Family

Sing!

Hello, Goodbye.

Hello, Goodbye.

Hi my friend.

Bye my friend.

Hello, Goodbye.

Exercises

A. Who is this?

Write a sentence. This is ....

1.
2.
3.
4.
5.
6.

B. Say he or she for each picture above

C. Fill in the gaps by writing words that will match in the groups

1. Banana, mango, banana, mango, ...
2. Knife, plate, knife, plate, ..., knife
3. morning, afternoon, ...

D. Draw: My family

1. Mother
2. Father
3. Sister
4. Brother

E. Talk

Who is this?

Mother

Father

Sister

Brother

Revision

A. Write the answer. Choose yes or no.

1. Ima is a girl  ....

2. This is a pencil  ....

3. This is a dog  ....

4. This is a bicycle  ....

5. This is a Table  ....

6. Are you a boy? ....

7. Are you a sister? ....

Unit 6 Rehema can read

Look! This is c. That is a. That is t.
c, a and t makes cat!

Look here! b!
b is for book. b is for bag. b is for ball.

d is for dog. d is for drum. d is for doll!

Come here! Here is f for flower.
Here is t for tree.

That is p for paper. This is m for me!

Here is the ALPHABET! I can read!

Sing the alphabet song!
a b c d e f g h i j k l m n o p q r s t u v w x y z
A B C D E F G H I J K L M N O P Q R S T U V W X Y Z

Exercises

A. Write the missing letters. Read

a	_	c	d	_	f	g	h	_	j	k	_	m
n	o	p	q	r	s	_	u	v	w	x	y	z

a	b	c	_	e	f	_	h	_	j	k	_	m
n	_	p	q	_	s	_	u	_	w	x	_	z

_	_	c	d	_	f	_	_	i	_	_	l	m
n	_	p	_	r	_	_	u	v	w	_	y	_

B. Find the Odd one Out.

a	a	a	o	a	a
e	e	c	e	e	e
g	g	g	q	g	g
c	o	c	c	c	c

C. Find the same letter.

c	t	s	c	a	d	n
m	h	o	d	r	a	m
t	s	n	n	t	c	r
s	t	o	r	m	s	d
o	a	o	t	r	h	l
l	l	s	m	o	a	n

D. Match Letters with Pictures.

d
r
t
f
g
b
c

Revision

Put in order.

Example: I fine am you thank = I am fine thank you

evening good ....
are you how ....
name my is ....
is name her ....

Sing!

aeiou, aeiou, aeiou
I know the vowels
aeiou

Unit 7 Let us Count

Count.

Read the numbers.

Football!

Amani and Zawadi are in Class One this year. Today Class One and Class Two are playing football. There are ten players. Amani scores a goal! Then Zawadi scores a goal. Amani scores again. That is three goals! Class One wins the match.

Answer the Questions

1. How many goals does Amani score?
2. How many goals does Zawadi score?
3. How many players are there?
4. How many balls are there?
5. Who is watching?

Exercises

A. Count and write the number in the gap.

1. I can count .... birds.

2. I can count .... dogs.

3. I can count ....cups.

4. I can count ....cow.

5. I can count ....bottles.

B. There are / There is.

1. How many cats are there? There are ……….. cats.

2. How many hens are there? There are ……… hens.

3. How many bicycles are there? There is …………. bicycle.

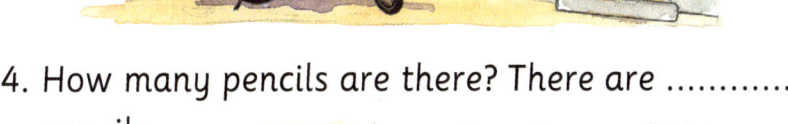

4. How many pencils are there? There are …………. pencils.

5. How many tables are there? There is ……….. table.

C. For more than one, add s!

1 book	2 books	1 tree	8 ....
1 dog	2	1 ball	5 ....
1 house	4	1 goal	7 ....
1 pencil	3	1 teacher	6 ....
1 desk	10	1 pupil	9 ....

Sing!

10 green bottles were standing on a wall.

A big wind blew and one fell down.

9 green bottles were standing on a wall.

A big wind blew and one fell down.

8 green bottles were standing on a wall.....

Revision

A. Fill in the gaps. Use these words.

rulers, pencils, balls, desks, cows, blackboard, girl, boy.

1. In the classroom there is one ....
2. In the classroom there are .... , ... and ....
3. Faraja is a ....
4. Zawadi is a........................ .

B. Put in order

1. a   d   c   b   e
2. l   p   m   o   n
3. l   j   i   c   h
4. u   v   t   w   s

C. Complete the sentences

is   am   are

1. I .... a pupil.
2. He .... my brother.
3. You .... my friend.
4. She .... my teacher.
5. I .... 7 years.

D. **Answer the Question.**

1. How many sisters do you have?
2. How many brothers do you have?
3. How many friends do you have?

Sound

1. Find the b words.

2. Find the p words.

Unit 8 Cat and Mouse

Cat and Mouse

Brown is a cat.
He is on the chair.

Mouse is behind
the door

There is bread
under the table.
Mouse runs there

Brown cat sees
Mouse.

Brown Cat jumps
under the table.
Mouse runs behind
the basket.

Brown Cat jumps in
front of the basket.
Mouse runs.

Brown Cat runs behind
the mouse.

Cat catch the mouse.

Sing!

Lazy, Brown cat
Lazy, Brown cat
See how he runs
See how he runs
He jumps on the little Mouse
Who runs to his little house
Have you ever seen such a lazy cat
Like lazy, Brown cat

Exercises

A. Where is it?

Fill in the gaps

in   on   behind   in front of   under

1. Mouse is .... the door.
2. Brown Cat is .... the table.
3. Mouse is .... the table.
4. Brown Cat is .... the table.
5. Mouse is .... the basket.
6. Brown Cat is .... the basket.
7. mouse is .... the hole.

B. Write the answer

Match the words to the Pictures
Use each word two times

in   on   behind   in front of   under

C. Write the answer

1. How many books are on the table?
2. How many books are on the chair?
3. How many bananas are on the table?
4. How many bananas are in the basket?
5. How many pencils are under the table?
6. How many mangoes are in the basket?

Sound!

J   Z

Unit 9 The Kitten and her Milk

May I?

May I drink this milk please?

No, you may not.

Because the milk is hot.

May I drink it now?

Yes, you may.

Thank you!

Break time

Rehema: Please, sir.
Teacher: Yes, Rehema?
Rehema: May I go home?
Teacher: No, you may not.
Rehema: Why?
Teacher: Because is not home time.
Rehema: May I play?
Teacher: Yes, you may. Take this ball.
Rehema: Thank you, sir.

Exercises

A. Look at the picture. Copy and fill in the gaps.

1. May I play with the ball?
   Yes, ... may.

2. May I cross the road?
   No, you .... not.

3. May I eat this banana?
   ...., you may not.

4. May I go out?
   No, ... may not.

5. May I read this book?
   Yes, you ....

B. What are they saying?

Revision

A. Write the names of the things on pictures.

1. 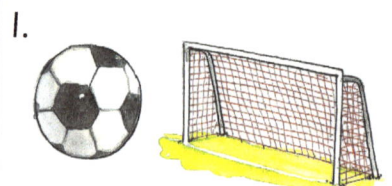	2. 
3. 	4. 
5. 	6. 

B. Use the right word to fill the gap

1. Rehema is number .... two
   ten

2. Zawadi can ....play
   read

3. She...........................runs to school
   walks to school

4. That is an............................orange
   egg

5. This is a............................rulers
   ruler

6. These are...........................birds
   bird

7. This is a..........................bag
   bags

A poem

The cat knocks, rat-a-tat-tat.

Mother says who is that?

It's me, pussy cat!

What do you want, pussy cat?

Some milk, please.

Where is your cup asks mother?

I left it with my brother.

Oh, you silly pussy cat!

Sound !

Match

m

n

Unit 10 The Lost Goats

Father says, Can you count the goats? How many do we have? asks Faraja. We have 25, says father. Faraja counts all the goats. There are only 19! 6 goats are not there! He looks for the goats. They are not at home.

Rehema comes. Faraja says, 6 goats are not here! Rehema says, Come, my friend. Let us look at school. At school they find 4 goats. Faraja says, Those are my goats!

Faraja takes them home. Now there are 23 goats. Then 2 goats come home. Faraja says, Those are the other 2 goats! Now there are 25 goats at home. Whew!

Balloons!

Can you count from one to twenty-five?

1 one	2 two	3 three	4 four	5 five
6 six	7 Seven	8 eight	9 nine	10 ten
11 eleven	12 twelve	13 thirteen	14 fourteen	15 fifteen
16 sixteen	17 seventeen	18 eighteen	19 nineteen	20 twenty
21 twenty one	22 twenty two	23 twenty three	24 twenty four	25 twenty five

Exercises

A. Count and Write.

Example:

   3   and   8   is   11

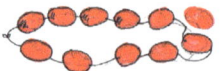 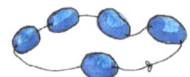 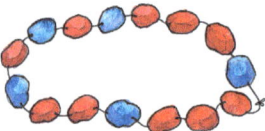

.... and .... is ....

.... and .... is ....

.... and .... is ....

These / Those

Example: These are near. Those are far.

Those are trees.

These are flowers.

Those are birds.

These are cats.

B. Answer and Count.

Example: What are these?
These are balls.
How many are there?
There are twelve balls.

1. What are these?
   These are ....
   How many are there?
   There are ....

2. What are these?
   These are ....
   How many are there?
   There are ....

3. What are these?
   These are ....
   How many are there?
   There are ....

4. What are those?
   Those are ....
   How many are there?
   There are....................

5. What are those?
   Those are ....
   How many are there?
   There are ....

6. What are these?
   These are ....
   How many are there?
   There are ....

C. Write the number in words.

17	....	25	....
18	....	16	....
21	....	11	....
24	....	12	....
19	....	14	....
13	....	23	....
15	....	20	....
22	....		

D. What is in the picture?

Read!

One, two, tie my shoe
Three, four, knock on the door
Five, six, pick up sticks
Seven, eight, lay them straight
Nine, ten, a big fat hen

Sound !

Find the matching sounds

k

g

Unit 11 Lion and Mouse

Read the story.

This is Lion.
He walks in the forest.

He steps in a net!

He cannot get out.

Mouse comes.
She sees Lion.
Good morning Mouse,
says Lion.

Mouse says, good morning Lion. Why are you in the net?

I cannot get out, says Lion. Please help me.

I am afraid. You will eat me! says Mouse. Why are you in the net?

No, I will not eat you. Please help! says Lion.

What can I do? thinks Mouse. I can chew the net.

Mouse chews the net lion gets out.

Thank you, Mouse! says Lion. You are welcome, says Mouse.

Answer the questions

Yes / No

1. Does Mouse chew the net?
2. Does Lion eat Mouse?
3. Does Lion say thank you?
4. Is Lion happy to get out of the net?
5. Can a small animal help a big animal?

Act out the Lion and the Mouse.

Exercises

A. Put in order.

Example: cna - can

1. em ....
2. ouy ....
3. og ....
4. eys ....
5. loin ....
6. ays ....
7. etg ....
8. otu ....

B. Write the missing letter.

Example: l _ ion - lion

1. b a _ l
2. c _ n
3. w _ n
4. _ o r n i n g
5. n _ t
6. m o u _ e

C. Choose the Right Answer.

Can / Cannot put ✓ or ✗

A mouse can chew the net.

A mouse can eat a lion.

A mouse can run.

mouse can jump.

A mouse can score a goal.

Can / Cannot put ✓ or ✗

A lion can run.

A lion can play football.

A lion can eat.

A lion can read.

A lion can jump.

D. Making Questions.

To make a question, turn the words around like this:

This is a lion.   —   Is this a lion?
That is a net.   —   Is that a net?

Make questions.

1. This is a mouse.............................
2. That is a football............................
3. These are players............................
4. Those are balloons..........................
5. That is a ruler................................
6. These are kittens............................
7. This is a pencil. ....
8. Those are drums............................
9. That is a hen.................................
10. This is a book...............................

Play the game Twenty Questions with a Friend.

Sound !

Write and draw three words that start with t:
example: tree

Write and draw three words that start with d:
example: drum

Unit 12 Let us Play a Game

Amani: Let's play a game.
Zawadi: Yes. Let's play Follow the Leader.
Faraja: I am the leader.

Sit down.

Stand up.

Turn around.

Play Follow the Leader!

Sing!

Stand up, sit down
Stand up, sit down
Jump, Jump, Jump
Stand up, sit down

Exercises

A. Match picture with word

a.   1. clap

b.   2. jump

c.   3. stand

d.   4. turn around

e.   5. sit down

B. **Fill in the gaps**

turn, come, stand, sit.

1. .... up, Amani.
2. John, ... down.
3. Zawadi, ... around.
4. ....here, Anna.

B. **What are they saying?**

Sound !

l / r   Name these and match.

Unit 13 Days of the Week

\	January 2007					
Monday	Tuesday	Wednesday	Thursday	Friday	Saturday	Sunday
1	2	3	4	5	6	7
8	9	10	11	12	13	14
15	16	17	18	19	20	21
22	23	24	25	26	27	28
29	30	31				

On Monday,
the ants eat sugar.

On Tuesday,
the ants eat a banana.

 On Wednesday, the ants eat fish.

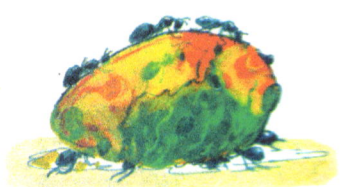 On Thursday, the ants eat a mango.

 On Friday, the ants eat a cake.

 On Saturday, oh no!

 On Sunday, the ants stay home.

Exercises

A. Put the days of the week in order.

1. Monday
2. Tuesday
3. Sunday
4. Wednesday
5. Saturday
6. Friday
7. Thursday

B. Fill in the days

I am thinking of a day
It starts with................

1. M................
2. Th................
3. W................
4. Sa................
5. Tu................
6. F................
7. Su................

Revision

A. Yes or no?

1. A mouse can clap.
2. A cat can sit down.
3. A table can turn around.
4. A pencil can jump.
5. A teacher can stand.

B. Write the numbers and put in order

1.
Five
Twenty
Fifteen
Twenty five
Ten

2.
Two
Six
Eight
Twelve
Four
Ten

C. Sounds!

Match

f   v

Unit 14 Amani and the Rabbit

Amani: Hello, Rabbit, how are you?

Rabbit: Fine, thank you Amani.

Amani: Tell me, rabbit, what do you do everyday?

Rabbit: Oh, I hop, I jump. I run all day long.

Amani: Do you eat everyday?

Rabbit: Yes, I eat carrots and green leaves.
Tell me, Amani, what do you do everyday?

Amani: Every morning I wake up. I take a bath. I brush my teeth. I comb my hair. I put on my clothes and drink tea. I go to school.

Rabbit: Do you brush your teeth everyday?

Amani: Yes. This is the song for morning.

> This is the way
> I brush my teeth
> Brush my teeth
> Brush my teeth
> This is the way
> I brush my teeth
> Early in the morning.

Rabbit: That is a nice song!

Exercises

A. Put in order.

He takes a bath.

He wakes up.

He goes to school

He drinks tea.

He combs his hair

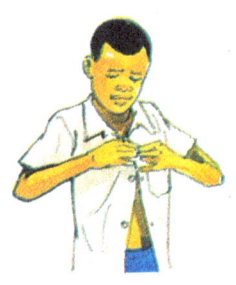
He put on clothes

He brushes his teeth

B. Who does it?

Complete the sentences. Choose Amani or Rabbit.
1. .... hops and runs everday.
2. .... brushes his teeth in the morning.
3. .... eats carrots and leaves.
4. .... goes to school.
5. .... sings a song.

C. Match the pictures with sentences.

1.

   a. He counts goats every evening.

2.

   b. He sleep in the bed every night.

3.

   c. It drinks milk everyday.

4.

   d. He runs home every afternoon.

5.

   e. She reads a book everyday.

D. Choose the right one

Example: She (jump/jumps).
Answer: She jumps.

1. I (eat/eats)
2. You (sleep/sleeps)
3. I (read/reads)
4. She (run/runs)
5. He (count/counts)
6. You (sing/sings)

C. Sounds!

2 sounds of C. Find the sounds.

Unit 15 Count to Fifty

Rehema's sister Flora is in a race. It is a big race. It is fifteen kilometers long. She is number forty two. There are fifty people in the race. Every runner has a number.

Flora is very fast. She wins!

Counting twenty six - fifty
Remember numbers one - nine?

1 one	4 four	7 seven
2 two	5 five	8 eight
3 three	6 six	9 nine

Now count:

20 twenty
30 thirty
40 forty
50 fifty

Put them together:

21 twenty-one
25 twenty-five
28 twenty-eight
32 thirty-two
47 forty-seven

Zawadi is counting from twenty one to thirty. help her count.

Faraja and Rehema can count from thirty up to fifty.

Count from thirty to fifty.

30 thirty	41 forty one
31 thirty one	42 forty two
32 thirty two	43 forty three
33 thirty three	44 forty four
34 thirty four	45 forty five
35 thirty five	46 forty six
36 thirty six	47 forty seven
37 thirty seven	48 forty eight
38 thirty eight	49 forty nine
39 thirty nine	50 fifty
40 forty	

Exercises

A. Fill in the gaps

Example: Mr. Kitini is number thirty - five

1. Rehema is number ....
2. Faraja is number ....
3. Amani is number ....
4. .... is number forty-four
5. Mr. Kitini is number ....

B. Write in words or numbers

27 ....
.... thirty
48 ....
49 ....
.... twenty-six

50 ....
.... thirty-three
32 ....
41 ....
.... forty-four

C. Crossword

Fill in the names of the numbers in the puzzle.

Down:
1. 50
2. 22
3. 31
6. 30

Across:
1. 45
4. 26
5. 42
7. 40

D. Sounds!

Match

w

y

Unit 16 What is Happening?

Netball

It is afternoon. The pupils are playing netball. Faraja and Rehema are playing.

Rehema is number 2. Faraja is number 4. Amani and Zawadi are watching. Amani is happy. He is clapping. Faraja throws the ball to Rehema. Rehema scores a goal! One point for Rehema! Her team is winning! Look at the score!

What are they doing? Match the word with the picture

1.    The pupils are playing netball.

2.    Zawadi is singing.

3.    Amani is eating.

4.    Faraja is throwing a ball

5.    Rehema is jumping

Exercises

A. Add --- ing

Example: throw - throwing

1. go
2. jump
3. stand
4. open
5. turn
6. play
7. walk
8. read

B. Fill in the gaps

Remember: I am, You are, He is, She is, They are.

1. She ………………….. walking.
2. You ………………….. jumping.
3. I ……………………… singing.
4. He …………………… standing.
5. The girls ……………… catching.
6. The boys ……………… clapping.
7. The teacher ……………. looking.
8. They …………………. opening the door.
9. I ………………………. throwing the ball.
10. You ………………….. playing.

C. Match words with pictures

Example:  Climbing

a.  b.  c.

d.  e.  f.

eating   writing   reading   jumping   drawing   sleeping

Sounds!

s / h Find the odd ones out.

Revision

A. Find the word

   shoe   tree   three   milk

   table   dog   goat   girl

   pencil goal   race   ruler

   stone   she   shoe   soda

   banana mangoe Papaya tomato

   lion   mouse   cat   goat

B. Fill in the gaps

| am | is | are |

1. I ....in standard one
2. Rehema .... a girl.
3. Mr. Kitini .... a teacher
4. You ....very nice.
5. The hen .... eating.
6. You .... writing.

C. Finish the sentence

1. Pupil numbe 2 is ....
2. Pupil numbe 24 is ....
3. Pupil numbe 11 is ....
4. Pupil numbe 37 is ....
5. Pupil numbe 6 is ....
6. Pupil numbe 48 is ....
7. Pupil numbe 58 is ....

Standard One Keywords

Aa
afternoon
all day
ant
at home

Bb
baby
bag
ball
banana
basket
bath
behind
bench
bicycle
blackboard
book
bottles
boy
brother
bucket

Cc
cake
can
cannot
car
carry
cat
chair
chew
clap
class
climb
cold
count

Dd
day
deer
desk
dog
doll
down
drum

Ee
eight
eighteen
eleven
evening
excuse me

Ff
fast
father
fifteen
fine thank you
fish
five
flower
football
four
fourteen
friday
friend

Gg
garden
gate
girl
go
goal
goat
good
goodbye

Hh
hair
he
hello
help
hen
her
hi
his
hole
hot
hop
hot
house
how are you

Ii
i
in
in front of

Jj
jug
juice
jump

Kk
kitten
knife

Ll
leaves
leopard
lion

Mm
make
mango
market
may
me
milk
morning
mother
mouse

Nn
name
net
netball
nine
nineteen
no
not
number
numbers

Oo
on
one
open

Pp
paper
pencil
picture
palte
play
player
please

Rr
race
ride
ruler
run

Ss
saturday
score
seven
seventeen
she
shoe
shop
shut
sit
six
sixteen
sleep
soda
sometimes
stand
stone
stop
sugar
sunday
sweet

Tt

table
tea
teacher
teeth
telephone
ten
thank you
thanks
these
thirteen
those
three
throw
thursday
tomatoes
toothbrush
tree
tuesday
turn around
twelve
twenty
twenty-five
twenty-four
twenty-one
twenty-three
twenty-two
two

Uu

up

Ww

walk
watch
wednesday
week
where
who
win
window

Yy

yes
you
you are welcome

www.ingramcontent.com/pod-product-compliance
Lightning Source LLC
Chambersburg PA
CBHW041530220426
43671CB00003B/43